Abuse of Power

By Johnny Mack

Abuse of Power

Who is the real enemy?

A true story

By Johnny Mack

INKWELL PRODUCTIONS
Scottsdale, Arizona

First printing June 2010

ISBN: 978-0-9786202-2-6
Library of Congress Control Number: 2010922295

Published by Inkwell Productions
10869 N. Scottsdale Road #103-128
Scottsdale, AZ 85254-5280

Tel. 480-315-3781
E-mail info@inkwellproductions.com
Website www.inkwellproductions.com

This book is based on a true story. Some names, places and details have been changed to protect the privacy of those involved.

Prologue

Table of Contents

Prologue

February 22 2008

I awoke this morning as federal prisoner number 4563259 in the United States of America federal correctional facility in Florence, Arizona. I am in a small cement room with three beds and two Mexican nationals who don't speak much English as cellmates. I have never been imprisoned before; much less arrested. I am a forty-year-old father of four and grandfather of three beautiful granddaughters. I have a wife to whom I've been married for 23 years.

My head is spinning from the last 48 hours and I am thinking, "how in the hell did this happen?"

As I lie here, staring at the gray, cracked ceiling, my thoughts wander back nearly 30 years, to where this story begins.

Abuse of Power

Chapter 1

First flight

October 2, 1978, Puerto Peñasco, Sonora, Mexico

"Listen to me Johnny I am going to keep this simple, if you can feel the wind on your face, you will live, but if at any time you can't feel the wind on your face, you are probably going to die." That was my Dad giving me my first lesson in the potential hazards of aerodynamic stall and preflight instruction in a motorized single seat ultralight aircraft that I was about to fly solo for the first time. I was eleven years old.

It was a warm sunny day on the beach in Puerto Peñasco, Mexico, and after a short pause to think about what I was going to do in the next few minutes, I pointed the aircraft into the wind and gave it full throttle. It accelerated slowly on the sand but within one hundred feet I was airborne! What an amazing feeling!

I kept the aircraft flying twenty feet above the beach and began to realize what life was about — flying. The smooth sea breeze, the soft white sand, the unspoiled and unoccupied beaches and the clear blue sea of Cortez lay beneath my wings. I thought I had died and gone to heaven and nearly did when I ran the aircraft out of fuel after being airborne for nearly thirty minutes. Thankfully the aircraft flew pretty well without the engine running and I was able to land "dead stick" right next to where Dad was standing. "Dead stick" means you continue to fly and land the aircraft without the engine running, which can be hazardous, but at the time I didn't think much about it. After the landing was over, Dad walked over and asked me why I would do something so stupid as running out of fuel in the air. I responded, "You didn't teach me anything about running out of fuel in your lesson." We both laughed, but much later I realized that I had learned an important lesson that day.

Soon I was flying the ultralight like a maniac all over the southwest United States and caught the attention of a Phoenix, Arizona, television station. They sent one of their television crews out to where we flew in Chandler, Arizona, and did a short TV segment about my flying that aired locally. Within a month, I received a call from the national television show "Kidsworld". They expressed interest in doing a story on my flying. "Kidsworld" sent out a film crew and they produced a thirty-minute show that aired nationally on TV. At age twelve I had my fifteen minutes of fame and was the youngest, most famous pilot in America.

I continued flying ultralights until my dad was nearly killed from a wing failure in one and he decided it was too dangerous for me too. As much flying as

I have done in my life, I still think about those early years flying down the beach in Mexico wearing nothing but a swimsuit and a big grin across my face. Dad taught me a lot of things in those years—work hard, play hard and dream big.

My parents had been high school sweethearts. Dad was born in California and Mom was born in Indiana. Both of their families had relocated to Phoenix, Arizona, for better work opportunities in the late 1950s. My mom and dad met at McClintock High School and married in Las Vegas just after graduating in the mid 1960s. Dad was pretty good at baseball and received a scholarship to college but soon learned he was no student. He continued to play baseball however and ended up on a semi-pro team for a while. After my mom became pregnant with me, she encouraged dad to pursue the family business of aerospace manufacturing, a business that he ended up doing pretty well.

I started walking at eight months and was riding motorcycles and driving go-karts by age three. My mom always worried about my many motorized activities at such a young age, but she admits I always had an uncanny ability to ride, drive and fly anything I climbed on. Like many other Arizona boys, I played baseball, football and swam on the swim team. My family was fairly well off and we were able to do a lot of outdoor activities such as racing motorcycles, water skiing, summering in San Diego and going to

Colorado or Utah for snow skiing in the winter. From a young age, I loved all things motorized and started racing motocross at eight years old. I raced and rode off-road motorcycles throughout the Southwest United States and Mexico until moving to Chicago, Illinois, in January 2009.

At age eight I was baptized in the Mormon Church and remain an active member to this day. I enjoyed school and earned pretty good grades but really didn't put a lot of effort into my schoolwork. In high school I was fairly popular and the defensive captain of the football team. One of the most important things I learned about prayer was from a football experience. You have to remember I was raised in a strict Mormon family and while racing motorcycles, flying hang gliders and other dangerous stunts were acceptable behaviors, our religion and especially prayer was not to be taken lightly and I had been instructed on how to pray from a young age.

Our football team's tradition was to pray before we left the locker room for the playing field a few minutes before game time. One of our coaches usually gave the prayers but on this night, which happened to be homecoming against our arch rival, one of our defensive players named Scott jumped up and volunteered to give the prayer. Scott was from what I would call an other-than-religious family, and his dad would often show up drunk to watch our practices during the week and more than once was thrown off the practice fields by our coaching staff because he could become fairly belligerent. I was very skeptical that Scott knew anything about praying. I was impressed however when he started the prayer by saying, "Dear God, thank you for the opportunity we have to play our arch rivals this night," but I became horrified as he continued, "and help us to kick their asses, Amen."

The whole locker room went dead silent as most of us fully expected a lightning strike to instantly destroy us. When that didn't happen, one of our coaches jumped up and yelled "Amen!" and the rest of us followed suit and charged out of the locker room like wild animals.

I started to think my parents were wrong about what to ask God for in a prayer because we went out and immediately recovered a fumble at the kickoff and scored a touchdown in the first minutes of the game. We were kicking their asses! It didn't last long however and my worst fears were confirmed as we proceeded to be beaten badly to the tune of 34-7. Lesson learned and duly noted.

As I look back at my high school years, I am most grateful to my parents for the upbringing I had and for the fact that I never felt like I needed to try drugs or alcohol.

I was always looking for a new adrenaline rush and was certainly able to experience many of them before I turned eighteen years old. I am an adrenaline junkie by nature and I know if I had tried alcohol or drugs they would have eventually destroyed me. Even without those addictions to contend with, I have been to the edge and looked down into the abyss more than a few times in my life, but as far as I know, that's where the biggest adrenaline rushes reside.

Chapter 2

Introduction

"Hey can we come over? I'm sneaking out tonight with my friend Jenny and we will be at your house in fifteen minutes!" That was one of my high school girlfriends calling me late one night. I am unknowingly just about to be introduced to my future wife.

Jenny was born in Mesa, Arizona the second of five children, to Frank and Karen Johansson, both from small towns in Idaho. Frank was a hardworking farmer's son who decided at a young age that farming just wasn't for him. In high school, he took an aptitude test and it showed that his interests lay in the electrical engineering field. Frank jokes now that he didn't know what an electrical engineer was at the time, but the test must have been right because he went on to get his degree in electrical engineering and was hired right out of college to work for the company now known as Medtronic. He helped pioneer much of the heart pacemaker and defibrillator technology we have today that has prolonged so many lives. Jenny's parents divorced about the time she was thirteen-years-old. Frank met another woman, Susan, who had four kids of her own, and they decided to become the Arizona version of the Brady Bunch. Karen also remarried. She met an attorney from LA by the name of Ira Schulman, and the two still live together in California. Jenny didn't have much in the way of material possessions in her early years due to how many children her father was supporting. She got along fairly well with her half brothers and sisters, even though there was some stress mixing the two families. She decided at a young age to follow the teachings of the Mormon Church. What I admired most about Jenny was that even as a young girl she wanted to be an example to her younger brothers and sisters who all looked up to her. I personally believe her mental and physical toughness come from those early years, a time that she had to be strong to survive.

When my girlfriend and Jenny arrived at my house that first night, I completely focused on every word Jenny said. Everything about her was amazing; she had beautiful blonde hair, a gorgeous smile and a great figure. Her voice simply made me melt and, even though I felt like I had nothing intelligible to say to her, she must have sensed my interest in her because before she left that night she slipped me her phone number. I couldn't wait to talk to her again so I called her that very night and we talked until the early morning hours. By the end of our conversation, I had asked her on a date and she thankfully accepted. Jenny lived with her family just a few streets down from my parents' house in the city of Scottsdale, Arizona. We attended the same high school as well as the same church. As the weeks turned into months we became a more serious couple. We were very young and in love and before much time went by our relationship became physical. Jenny called me on the phone one of those hot Arizona evenings in July and asked me to come over to her house. I drove over to her house wondering what could be so urgent. When I arrived she was waiting in her front yard and I could see on her face it was something serious. She climbed into my car and calmly said, "Johnny, I am pregnant." and then immediately broke down crying.

I was more shocked than scared but as the ramifications of what she said began to work through my mind, I became frightened. I managed to hold on to my emotions and promised her that I would be there and would not abandon my responsibilities. We spent a few hours talking and finally decided to wait for a few weeks, just to make sure she was indeed pregnant. After a few weeks passed and the store bought pregnancy test came up positive, we found ourselves at a crossroads of our young lives with a difficult decision to make. We decided not to tell our parents about the pregnancy, thinking it would be better to run away together. After eight weeks of indecisiveness about our future plans, we chose a Saturday night and told our parents we were going to a movie but actually loaded our things into my car and left Scottsdale.

It was terribly exciting to be on the run, to

be carefree and without any real direction for the future. All that mattered was that we were happy. We honeymooned for a few days in Southern California and then drove to Santa Monica to stay with Jenny's mom for a few days. Our parents were sick with worry and asked us to come back to Arizona to work things out. We did. Neither set of parents wanted us to get married, but after a long struggle, and realizing we weren't going to give in, they allowed us to marry on August 14, 1984.

I rented a small apartment in the city of Chandler, Arizona, and we both finished our senior year of high school while I worked to support us. We were poor, but we had each other, and we were happy. We did our best to stay independent from our families that first year. It wasn't that difficult to accomplish since our relationships with them were so strained. We knew they loved us, but we wanted to prove to them we could make it on our own. I think that even though it was stressful, it helped cement the bond Jenny and I had. Our daughter Kaylee was born in February 1985 and she was our pride and joy. Dad eventually helped me start my own Aerospace machine shop business, and when Jenny and I started to do a little better financially we had our second child, a son we named JR. We found ourselves at the age of eighteen with two children and a small business.

Chapter 3

The Aerospace business

I worked in the aerospace machine shop business from the time I was twelve-years-old. I guess my parents had never heard of child labor laws or worse knew about them but just didn't care. It turned out great for me because I learned the value of hard work at an early age. I worked at my Dad's company until he helped me start my own about a year after Jenny and I married. The aerospace business is a highly technical, competitive business and I had to learn it the hard way. Thank goodness for the computer age because the technology really changed manufacturing for the better. I started working in the business at a time when computer numeric controlled equipment, or CNC, was replacing the old manual methods of manufacturing. Between the computer and ever evolving machining software, smaller companies like us could produce quality parts in a very short time frame. I worked long hours, as many entrepreneurs do, and if it took me working thirty hours straight to get a job done, that's what I did. I worked hard and I played harder. My grandfather always said if I worked half as hard as I played I would be rich, and he probably wasn't far off from the truth. Being in manufacturing was a good business and afforded my family many luxuries that most people never get to enjoy. I was able to spend a lot of time motorcycle riding and racing off-road, and I really loved the competition. My company grew through the early 1990s, and about that time I met another business owner from Mesa, Arizona by the name of Dan Stapley who owned a company called Engine Trix. Dan was a few years older than me and was just as crazy as I was about motorized stuff. His company specialized in modifying motorcycles and jet skis and we had similar personal backgrounds. We hit it off right away. I began building parts for Dan's modified jet skis and motorcycles, and early in 1992, we developed an aftermarket line of products for the California Go-Ped, a gas powered, motorized scooter that became incredibly popular throughout the United States. If you bought a machined aluminum deck, billet aluminum wheels, a third bearing support or hardened roller drives, you most likely bought them from us. It was amazing how many parts we sold. We did so well that we soon had many other businesses copying our designs and selling them. Dan introduced me to jet ski racing and within two years I became the California State Runabout Class Jet Ski Champion and went on to win second place overall at the 1995 IJSBA Jet Ski World Finals, setting a world record in the slalom event.

Dan was a terrible diabetic and in 1996 had a liver

and pancreas transplant in the futile attempt to save his life. Dan fought hard but just never fully recovered from the transplant, although it bought him a few more months with his family. On February 20, 1997, at about two o'clock in the morning, old, Dan passed away at the age of forty-three, leaving behind four children and a wife. I got the news about Dan's passing the afternoon of February 21st and, although it was sort of expected, I didn't take it very well. When I got home from work that day, I told Jenny that I didn't even get to say good-bye to him. Jenny said, "Honey, don't you remember what happened last night? You were fast asleep in bed and suddenly you sat up and said, 'Good- bye Dan, I'll see you soon' I was awake reading and it scared me at first but you didn't say anything more so I let it go. You did say good bye to him." I believed her but I really had no recollection of it. Dan was a good friend, and I have a lot of good memories of being at the races with him and I do hope to see him again someday. I learned from Dan that even though the body is weak and can be broken and hurt, the spirit stays strong and makes you who you are and more importantly how you are.

By this time, I had lost interest in professional jet ski racing and, in January 1996, moved on to off road car racing. Dad and I bought our first off road race car in 1996 and immediately entered the Score Parker 400, a 400 mile long off road car race held in Parker, Arizona, run through some of the most rugged desert ever created. I started the race with 300 other racecars but I crashed very badly about halfway into the race. After a few hours, and with the help of our pit crew, we got the race car repaired enough to finish in tenth place and were immediately hooked. It takes a special breed of human to want to off road race as it is most likely the most hazardous motor sport event ever created. Imagine driving through very rough, unfamiliar terrain, up to 120 mph, in a dust cloud so thick you can only see the hood of your car. It is an amazing adrenaline rush, and for a certain few, there is nothing else.

Early in 1996 we met up with an off road race car builder out of San Diego, California, by the name of Matt Johnson, who owned a company called Jenco Race Cars. Matt was having trouble with the durability of some of his racecar suspension parts, and we immediately developed a new way to manufacture them, which he still uses today. We also designed, developed and produced a forged billet racing wheel for off road racing that remains the industry standard. We ended up buying one of Jenco's racecars and soon began having some success winning the Score San Felipe Baja 250, Score Laughlin race, Baja 500 and Baja 1000 in 1998. The aerospace business was going well, and, with our aftermarket sales also growing, we were really flying high. As well as we were doing, we discovered off road racing was becoming extremely expensive. Finally in 2001, we decided we had pretty well spent all the money we were going to spend racing.

As the year 1999 came around, we were advised by Honeywell, an aerospace company to which we supplied parts that constituted about half of our Aerospace business, to open a facility in a foreign low cost economic region. We looked at their list of countries and the closest one to Phoenix, Arizona, was Mexico. Dad didn't like the idea of operating a business in Mexico at all, and the more he thought about it the less he liked it. Mexico was where we went to play, not work, and he was well aware of the inherent difficulties we would have starting up a facility in Mexico. With Dad making his position on the subject known to everyone, I began to think about how I could do it on my own and without causing big problems between us. I knew that for our company to continue to have a future with Honeywell, this foreign facility project was necessary and I became determined to make it happen. I was nowhere near retirement and needed to secure my family's future. I took Honeywell's advice very seriously.

In one of the supplier meetings at Honeywell, I was pulled aside by a purchasing manager who told me, "Look Johnny, you are going to have to open up in Mexico soon and if you don't, you will have no more purchase orders for your United States facility."

His statement didn't surprise me too much but when I asked him why his response was a little more shocking. The purchasing manager told me that the tax breaks are so big from the United States government for companies like Honeywell to outsource work to emerging countries that they have no choice but to advise companies like mine to move out of the United States so they can take advantage of the tax breaks. I remember the purchasing manager saying it was a make or break deal for Honeywell and I left the meeting thinking that this was truly unbelievable. As I was driving home that day I knew I had a problem, knowing what my dad's position was, but also knowing our business was under a serious threat.

Through off road racing a few years before, I had met a fellow Honeywell supplier by the name of Jackie James. Jackie invited me to go with him to Guaymas in Sonora, Mexico, to attend a presentation by a company who provided foreign shelter services. We flew down in my plane to Guaymas, a town we were both pretty familiar with, and sat through the presentation. Maquiladoras, for those who are not familiar with the word, provide shelter services for foreign businesses that operate in Mexico. More specifically, they provide facilities, transportation, employees, tax services, legal counsel, foreign transition and operation. In other words, you effectively operate your business under their umbrella for a fee. I left the presentation thinking it was too expensive to pay to the shelter, and would wind up costing us more money to manufacture parts in

Mexico than in the United States. When I expressed my
concerns to Jackie, he agreed with me. No more than a
couple of weeks later he called me and said, "Johnny,
I signed a deal with the Maquila Group and if you go
run it I will put up the money to get it going and we can
split it fifty-fifty."

I thought about it for about two seconds and
said, "All right let's do it." The challenge of this new
adventure was tempting and I had no doubt that it was
good for the future. It was just after September 11,
2001, when I drove down to Mexico and started up
Precision Products de Mexico SA de CV in the city of
Empalme, Sonora. The task of opening a manufacturing
facility was one of the most difficult things I have ever
done, but in the end it all worked out, and the company
still remains in business today. I commuted down to the
plant every week using my own plane, a Mooney 252
TSE, a single engine four-seat piston engine airplane.
I would leave the Chandler, Arizona, airport at about
0500 and arrive in Guaymas Mexico around 0700 and
be in my office by 0730. Needless to say I was faced
with a monumental task. A manufacturing facility needs
many specially trained people, of which we had none.
I hired one aerospace engineer just out of college and
six fishermen, none of whom spoke English. Although
I knew some Spanish before I moved to Mexico, it
took me a few months to catch up with my employees'
communication levels and to make them fully

understand what I needed done. The language barrier was soon overcome, and my little group of seven buckled down and really went to work. By putting in eighteen-hour days, six days a week, we took an empty building and wired it, plumbed it for compressed air, got our Aerospace AS9002 quality system approved, moved in Computer Numerically Controlled manufacturing equipment and were producing aerospace parts, all in just six months. Inside of a year we had fifty employees and were turning a few heads in the Maquila industry. I will say that the Mexican people I hired were hard workers, dedicated and proud of their association with the company. I learned from them that it is much better to have hard, dedicated workers who really make an effort rather than raw talent that is too self-centered. We out produced our United States sister companies in both quality and on time delivery within nine months; this was accomplished with people who had never seen, heard or much less operated the type of sophisticated equipment we had in our plants. It was truly amazing to see their transition. We all worked so well together that we even started a company soccer team and proceeded to play in the Maquila leagues. I played with them, but I was definitely one of the weaker ones on the team.

Chapter 4

Aviation

In my life, I have experienced about every sort of motorized and non-motorized activity, and, in my humble opinion, aviation is the pinnacle of all human achievements.

Aviation is the world's fastest, most dangerous motor sport. Commuter flying is also safe and the average person's preferred method of transportation.

Even though the government has tried to legislate general and commercial aviation into oblivion, it is still the best means of travel. Within one hundred years, aviation has changed our lives and has made this planet much smaller. Suddenly it doesn't matter where your family, friends or clients live, you can be there in a short time. I have loved aircraft since the age of two when I would go flying in my Dad's Mooney and sit in his lap while we flew. An airplane is nothing more than a time machine, and a helicopter is the ultimate off road vehicle. Both can take you places, allow you to see things most people never dream of and afford you the luxury of getting to see the world from a whole new perspective. As you now know, I began my flying career at a very young age and never gave up on it.

Even when I was busy developing other businesses,
I constantly expanded my aviation base by earning
new ratings and flying new airplanes and helicopters.
I even did quite a bit of aircraft buying and selling on
the side. There is definitely some money to be made
selling aircraft, although, as most aircraft owners will
tell you, aviation is where you spend money not where
you make money. You fly aircraft because you love it
and you have to love it because it is costly. My father
and grandfathers always had airplanes around, and I got
my private pilot's license when I was seventeen years
old. Dad owned a Cessna T206 and a Bellanca Citabria
model 7ECA, which is a small two-person aerobatic
airplane. If you notice, Citabria spelled backward is
"airbatic," a play on the word aerobatic. Anyway, I
got my license in the Citabria and proceeded to take
aerobatic lessons. Every week I practiced loops, rolls,
hammerheads, Cuban 8s, inverted flight and the like
until I would nearly throw up. I took all my friends
and family that dared to go flying and made most of
them scream until we landed. I had a lot of fun with
that plane and am thankful for the opportunities I had
to fly it at such a young age. Dad also had a Cessna
Turbo 206. This plane had a Robertson STOL kit,
which stands for Short Take Off and Landing. With
these kits, you can take a fully loaded Cessna 206,
about 700 kilos of passengers, fuel and cargo, depart
from a 250 meter long, dirt runway, fly for a few hours

to another dirt runway of 250 meters in length and land
with no problem. This makes for a great ranch airplane,
which is what Dad used his for. Because of these STOL
characteristics, it also makes one of the best smuggling
airplanes ever created, which is why the Mexican drug
traffickers like them so much. Dad and I flew his T206
into his ranch in central Arizona many times where we
were only landing in pastures and small roads, and I
learned a lot from him about how to survive flying in
and out of small places. Dad was a pretty good stick
but had learned in the days before radio communication
was required. He was weak in that area and pretty
much quit flying once a radio and transponder were
required to fly in the Phoenix area. Back in the day, my
grandfather owned a couple of planes and had let my
father earn his pilot's license flying an Aeronca Champ
at the tender age of sixteen. Pilots all know what a
Aeronca Champ is, but for everyone else it is a small
fabric covered airplane with two tandem seats, a 65
hp engine and not much else; it is basically a stripped
down predecessor to the Citabria. Dad used to fly it to
the local lakes around the Phoenix area to land and take
off from the boat ramps. Of course, that was before
too many people thought that it was unsafe to do such
a thing; if you tried a stunt like that today, you would
go to jail and lose your pilot's license at the very least.
His most famous stunt, however, was while on a date
with his girlfriend, who later became my mom. Dad

had decided to fly at tree top level next to the Salt River and unexpectedly caught the landing gear in the top of a mesquite tree at 65 MPH. He literally flipped the plane over on its back, crashing it into the ground. This should have killed them both, but miraculously they both walked out of it – thank Goodness. I personally can't believe that Mom's father, also a pilot, didn't kill Dad right then and there. Grandpa had loved flying his whole life and shortly after he died, my grandmother told me his last wish was to fly alongside me in one of the jets I flew. I never told Grandma that the night he died I was flying a Learjet model 55 over the Caribbean Sea on a perfect, clear moonlit night and had somehow felt grandpa's presence in the cockpit there with me. I didn't actually learn that he passed away until the next day and as far as I am concerned, he got his wish.

Chapter 5

Charter Company

One of the issues we had at Precision Products de Mexico was getting our completed parts and assemblies to the United States in a timely manner. We did plenty of trucking by road, but it was slow and unreliable. I was flying back and forth between Mexico and Arizona a lot anyway so decided to purchase a 135 charter airline with the idea to begin flying our parts and freight up to Arizona.

A 135 charter airline operates much like the 121 airlines that are household names such as Delta or Southwest Airlines as they both carry passengers and cargo for hire. The difference lies mostly in aircraft size and scheduling. The larger aircraft such as a Boeing 737 or Airbus 320 are more likely to be found operating on a 121 certificate whereas a smaller jet such as a Learjet or citation jet are more apt to be found on a 135 certificate. Any aircraft smaller than a light jet, such as a Cessna 421 or Piper Navajo, is usually found operating on a 135 certificate if it is being used commercially for charter type flights.

I purchased Titan Air Corporation, a 135 charter airline owned by two airline captains who happened to be brothers, Mark and Mike Larson. They had started Titan Air to give them something to do after retiring out of the commercial airlines but had lost interest in running the business. I applied for Mexico's operating certificates and started running my manufacturing company's freight from Guaymas, Mexico. I also started building a charter clientele for my airplanes mostly consisting of fisherman, Baja California tourists and other businessman from the United States traveling to Mexico.

About this same time, the city of Mesa, Arizona, took over the decommissioned Williams Air Force Base, renamed it Williams Gateway airport and were actively looking for an income generating use for the airport. One of the options was international airfreight. Upon the city's discovery that I owned a company involved in international airfreight, I was invited to the airport commission meetings. I attended the airport commission meetings for a few months and it was decided I would fly the freight directly into Gateway airport from Mexico as the city was trying to gain publicity in the international freight-forwarding arena. It took me a few months to obtain the proper authority as the flight required special over flight permission from the department of Homeland security. At this time, September 11th was fresh in everyone's mind and I was a little worried how the first flight would go, so I flew it myself. After a slight scare with Tucson,

Arizona, approach controllers ordering me to land or
be intercepted by F-15 fighters, the proper person was
finally contacted and we were allowed to proceed on
to Gateway airport. The flight was locally covered
by television and newspaper reporters and was a big
deal to the city because it was the city's first ever
international flight arrival. I figured the free publicity
couldn't hurt me either.

Once word got around about the Titan Air Corp
international freight flying business, I received several
calls every week from various companies asking me to
sell Titan Air Corp to them. I finally sold in 2005 but
stayed on as chief pilot for a bit to help transition in
their people.

Abuse of Power

Chapter 6

Flying in Mexico

I can't even guess how many hours I have accrued flying around south of the United States border just above ground level through canyons and down beaches. I have several videos taken from inside the cockpits of different jets and turboprop aircraft, at ten feet off the deck and 400 mph. There is nothing funnier than buzzing over your friends' boat or house and knocking the shingles off of his roof or worse. You go to jail for that kind of stuff in the United States, but in Mexico, as long as nobody dies, it's all good. My friends and I called it low level hell because that's exactly what it was. At the Baja 1000 off road races, we would fly over the sea of Cortez ten miles out from the shoreline and head for a friend's RV or house near the beach a few feet above the water. The force of a small jet going by at 400 mph is substantial and I can't count how many tents, beach umbrellas, people and lounge chairs we would knock over when we flew over them.

A charter client of mine had a fishing yacht down in La Paz, Mexico, and in one of our visits to his yacht we caught his crewmembers off guard. It was late afternoon as we arrived from the United States for a fishing trip, and we dropped in on his yacht from 10,000 feet. We flew so close to the yacht that the force of our low fly-by knocked the captain right off of the boat and into the sea. My client thought it was the funniest thing he had ever seen, but the captain was slightly less amused and I was just glad the boat wasn't moving. I did all sorts of flying in Baja, including helicopter flying. Baja is an amazing piece of real estate with 12,000ft peaks, barren desert and lush coastal gardens all within an hour's flight; it is a bush pilot's dream. Fairly unspoiled and lawless, I pulled off more than a few stunts there. I had another client who insisted on being dropped off at a certain airstrip south of Ensenada, Mexico, which was marked on the aeronautical charts as a military base. I told him I would do it but that I couldn't stop there, and that he was on his own once he hit the ground. He agreed on the terms so I snuck him onto the airstrip at dusk without getting noticed, or so I thought. I pushed him and his gear out of the plane while it was still rolling and I quickly made a 180-degree turn and pushed in the throttles. I didn't like what I saw through the front windshield. I could see about twenty armed soldiers running across the airfield to stop me. I lifted off just in front of them as they started firing their rifles at me. I immediately did a hard left turn so they could only see the back of the aircraft from the ground and they wouldn't be able to identify the aircraft tail number. As I looked back at the runway my client was not in a good position. In fact, it looked like a scene from a war movie where the enemy is on all sides surrounding a lone combatant soldier whose death is imminent. The Mexican Military was surrounding my client from every direction and I could only hope the best for him. Adios my friend, vaya con Dios! I proceeded on to Ensenada without incident other than a few new holes in the airplane. I got a call from him a few days later and he said he was all right and they only kept him one night in jail. I hope it was worth it.

Many times at the Baja 1000 races you need to get into places where you have no runway and, if you don't have a helicopter, the only place to land is on the highway. This can be tricky and it is much safer to have a few guys on the ground to block automobile traffic for you. I have landed many aircraft on every sort of surface you can think of including those public highways. A few years back, my sons and I were taking our annual flying pilgrimage down to San Juanico, better known as Scorpion Bay, for our mens' surf trip, but when we arrived there we saw that the runway had been dug up by the federalies and was unusable. Unknown to most people, Scorpion Bay is a long, easy right break that rolls into a large bay offering amazingly long rides. It is one of the best spots to surf in the western hemisphere, and it is in the middle of nowhere. When I say it had a runway, I use the term very lightly because it wasn't much more than a dirt road. After finding the runway unsuitable, I made a few low passes over the beach and found some hard sand to land on. We landed without incident, dragged the plane up high on the beach and left it there. We tore it up in the waves for a few days and when it was time to leave, I discovered a small problem. The tide had risen and our beach "runway" was gone. I knew we couldn't takeoff on the soft sand, so we spent several hours collecting plants, driftwood and garbage to make a runway suitable for takeoff. We built ourselves about 300 meters of runway and it was barely enough to get our Cessna 185 airborne. After the initial thrill we had a smooth ride home.

Not too many people really understand the term adrenaline junkie, but I do. Part of the adrenaline junkie's rush is being able to outsmart the activity, so while I would not condone throwing oneself off of a high cliff, I would certainly give it the go ahead if there was some planning involved, like wearing a parachute. My point is there is a difference between suicidal activity and high-risk activity. I have always jokingly told my friends, "Anything that can't potentially kill you just isn't that much fun." I am a firm believer that it is never tragic to die doing what you love, but I know many people might think that's crazy or stupid. What's really tragic is dying before you have had the opportunities to accomplish your dreams. However, I had to learn the hard way about other boundaries that shouldn't be crossed.

During my work in Mexico I met all types of people and had every kind of flight request imaginable. For example, I would have clients that would request to be flown down to Mexico on a fishing trip. When we arrived at the location where the fishing trip was to begin, the clients would ask me to fly empty to another location, pick up their girlfriends and bring them back to the "fishing" location. After a week or so of "fishing," I would get the call to fly down there and take everybody back to where they came from. This is all fine on the outset, but most of the clients were married, of course, to other people. I would take the girls back home and then return to take my clients back to their homes and wives in the United States or Mexico. It happened all the time and eventually affected me as well. The very thought of getting away with something so seductive became a huge temptation. In retrospect, I know it was stupid because I would be risking my family, my money, my marriage and my integrity for some cheap thrills.

Chapter 7

Airplane theft in Mexico

The thing to remember about aircraft transactions is that you are selling to a world market, not a local one, thereby increasing your chances of encountering some shady characters. Most of the people I sold airplanes to were decent people, but even so you have to watch every detail of the transaction. One such transaction changed my life.

I had been buying and selling aircraft for many years, but the huge economic upswing in the years after September 11, 2001, had me in high gear with flipping aircrafts. Flipping means that you buy an aircraft mainly for the purpose of reselling it. In August 2005, I began receiving phone calls from an English speaking male who identified himself as Mark Smith from Sand Point, Idaho, an aircraft buyer interested in purchasing a Cessna T210 Centurion airplane. The Cessna T210 is very much like the Cessna T206 except that is has retractable gear and is about 40 knots faster at cruising speeds. Even though the Cessna T210 model hasn't been built since 1986, it is still an extremely sought after airplane in general aviation because of its versatility. It has virtually the same short takeoff and landing capability as the Cessna T206. Mark seemed to know quite a bit about the Cessna T210 model, and, much later, I discovered how he knew about them. He was a United States of America Drug Enforcement Agency (DEA) agent trying to set me up, which he eventually did.

I had a number of conversations with Mark by telephone, and we began to develop a business relationship. When he first called I owned a Cessna T210 like he was looking for, but it wasn't ready for sale as it was still being repaired and refurbished. I told Mark that I would have a Cessna T210 ready to sell in a few months and to keep in touch with me. Mark told me that he had a friend, new to aviation, that lived in Sand Point, Idaho, near him who also owned a vacation home near Hermosillo, Sonora, Mexico, and wanted to purchase the Cessna T210 to fly back and forth between his houses. He had enlisted Mark to help him with the buying process. This is actually a fairly common practice in aviation; you have someone who has a little money but doesn't know much about airplanes, he earns his private pilot's license, he then wants to buy his own airplane and he asks a friend who is more familiar with airplanes to walk him through the purchase process. Mark seemed like a decent guy, and I generally take people at their word. Up to this point I thought I could pick out tire kickers and bad guys, but boy was I wrong.

A few months went by and the Cessna T210 was

finished. I tested it myself by flying it around on various business flights. At this point I hadn't heard from Mark for a while but wasn't really worried because I knew plenty of potential buyers. I had been flying the Cessna T210 for a few weeks when Mark finally called me and asked if I could show the aircraft. We decided to set up an appointment for him and his buyer to view the airplane.

I told Mark that I had just sold another airplane, a single engine Mooney TLS, and was going to deliver it to the buyer the next day. I would be available anytime after that to show the Cessna T210. He said that would be fine and asked me if I would be willing to fly the T210 to a small airstrip just outside of Hermosillo, Mexico, on my next trip to Guaymas for the showing, which I refused to do. I have a policy to only meet a potential buyer, one that I haven't met in person, at an international or a fairly busy airport. In retrospect that should have been the first red flag, but Mark had been pretty straight with me the whole time and I had no real reason to distrust him. I told him I would be happy to show him the plane at the Hermosillo International airport which he said would be fine but they would be driving in from about two hours away by car. The fact that I had not personally met Mark and had only spoken with him on the phone would seem a little risky to some, but you have to remember that I grew up in the Sonora desert and that the southwest area of the United

States and Mexico are my backyard. Mark's request that I come to an out of the way airstrip was a little suspect, but I shrugged it off, which ended up being a costly oversight.

Mark and I had agreed to meet at the Hermosillo Sonora Mexico airport at 1500 hours on October 10, 2005, so I could show him and his friend the airplane. I departed in the Cessna T210 from Arizona and flew to Hermosillo, Mexico, arriving shortly after 1500 to meet with them. After closing my flight plan with the airport authorities, I discovered they had not yet arrived at the airport. At 1540 Mark called me on my cell phone and claimed they had been delayed and were still two hours away. Not a good start for these guys, I thought. I told him it would be no problem to wait, but he suggested we meet at 0900 the next day. I had planned to fly to Puerto Peñasco the next day anyway to check on a restaurant that I owned at the time, so I agreed. Mark apologized for the delay and I told him that I understood. I decided to proceed on to Guaymas, Mexico, that afternoon to spend the night in my house there.

October 11, 2005

At 0700, I went into the aerospace manufacturing plant in Guaymas to check on the work there and then returned to the Guaymas airport, filed a flight plan and

flew back to Hermosillo. I arrived about 0845, taxied
the plane right up to the front of the Airport Authorities
Offices and parked it in front of a large window that
has a direct view to the ramp. Again, no sign of Mark.
I decided to give him thirty minutes before I was going
to give up and fly to Puerto Peñasco. I got as far as
filing the flight plan before Mark finally called and said
they were running late but would be there in an hour.
In retrospect, another red flag. I gave him the benefit of
the doubt because I was a little hungry. I grabbed a taxi,
ran into town and ate a quick breakfast. I returned to
the airport about an hour later and my airplane wasn't
where I had left it. I knew everybody at the Hermosillo
airport and I just figured they had towed it to transient
parking to make room for other aircraft arrivals. I
looked around a bit and didn't see it, so I asked one of
the airport inspectors to assist me. We drove around the
entire airport looking for my plane. We searched every
hangar until we finally came upon the PGR's (Mexican
DEA) hangar, which had an armed guard in front of it.
The inspector told the guard he needed to see inside
the hangar and the guard refused the request. I knew
my plane was in there. The inspector then told me we
needed to see the airport commandant. At this point
I was getting a little worried, but I was still confident
that I would get my plane back. I knew Commandant
Estudillo well, and he had always been decent to me.
A commandant at a Mexican airport is God, and if you

need or want something you go to him. He can approve all sorts of things that aren't legal even in Mexico, including night operations even if the airport is closed, new business and anything else aviation related. I walked into Estudillo's office and I could see on his face that I was in trouble. He said, "John I fear that you will never see your airplane again." I requested him to make a report about the incident of my airplane being stolen from the airport, as he was obliged to do. He completed the report in Spanish and gave me a stamped copy. Estudillo and I went up to the control tower to make another report of the theft so it could be broadcast to nearby Mexican airports to keep a look out for my stolen aircraft. We also checked the tower records to see if any Cessna airplanes had left. None had. I then walked over to the Hermosillo police station, across the street from the airport, and made another report of the theft. I also called my aircraft insurance broker and advised him of the situation. My broker said not to worry it would be taken care of but added that I should make sure I have copies of all the reports. I was unable to get a commercial flight back to Phoenix that afternoon, so I checked into a hotel just a few blocks from the airport.

At this point I was certain that I'd been had by this man named Mark and his accomplices. I decided to call Mark's cell phone once again. I somehow knew that my calls were in vain, that he wouldn't answer, and of course he didn't, and my suspicions were confirmed.

I have many friends in the Hermosillo area, and I put out the word about my stolen plane. It didn't take long before a concerned friend knocked on my door and said, "John you need to leave Mexico now. The plane was taken by some very bad people that are saying they are going to kill you if you don't leave Hermosillo soon, and you are not safe here right now."

I told him, "Look my friend, this is my home and generally speaking, I feel safer here than anywhere else in the world. Besides what the hell have I done?"

He warned me once again and left in a hurry. I spent a sleepless night in the hotel, and the next morning I flew home on a commercial airline. Once I got home I tried to make sense of the whole situation. I didn't have any real enemies in Mexico, none that I knew of anyway, so the question was, why did this happen?

Things began to become clearer three days later when I received a phone call from another friend in Mexico saying, "Johnny, I just saw your Cessna T210 outside at the Hermosillo Mexico airport. It is now painted in the PGR's paint scheme and colors, the seats are stripped out of it and two American guys just got in it and flew it away."

PGR stands for Procuraduría General de la República. It is the Mexican equivalent of the United States Drug Enforcement Agency.

Immediately my suspicion was that was that my airplane was to be used to transport drugs up to the United States' borders. Since I was certain that my airplane would be coming back to Hermosillo, I sent five hundred dollars to my friend for detailed photos of my Cessna T210. I received the pictures about a month later. My friend put his life on the line to take the photos because if the wrong people saw him doing it, he would be dead. In the photos I received, the serial numbers of my airplane were clear.

Now, without a shadow of a doubt, my suspicions were confirmed. I also knew that the two American guys who flew the plane that day were DEA agents. This may come as a surprise to some American citizens but the US DEA is not necessarily an organization of good guys. It is an organization that is allowed to run wild all over the world in the name of stopping the flow of drugs across United States' borders. It is one of the most corrupt organizations the world has ever known, and it keeps proving it over and over again. Many of their agents and operatives commit theft, murder and just about every other atrocity known to man. What most United States citizens don't comprehend is that the DEA doesn't really want to stop the flow of drugs into the United States; they only want to control it. I don't have to tell you that illegal narcotics is a big business, and big business, illegal or not, most likely begets corruption. With big business just about everyone has a price and the DEA and the illegal drug traffickers both have theirs.

Of course on American television you see huge drug busts by the DEA almost every week. These are simply offerings to keep the population satisfied that someone is doing something about the war on drugs, as well as to justify the existence of the DEA. I will tell you that when not enough dope makes it across the USA borders to satisfy demand, the DEA and the PGR are happy to help out—for a fee, of course. The constant threat of trafficking is job security for these people, and you better believe they don't want to lose their livelihood. On more than one occasion, I have witnessed US government aircraft, in foreign countries, moving illegal substances in broad daylight. Who knows what they are up to at night. The DEA loves to put out horror stories for the press about traffickers and drug lords like Chapo Guzman of Sinaloa or the Felix brothers of Tijuana, but the truth is that the DEA does all the same things that they accuse the traffickers of doing. Without a doubt drug traffickers exist and they are very dangerous people, but, because of my personal experiences, I am far more afraid of my own government than I am of any Mexican drug lord. By the end of this book you will understand why.

Abuse of Power

Chapter 8

The insurance claim

A few days after I returned to Arizona from Hermosillo, Mexico, and the theft of my Cessna T210, I received a call from Joe Miller, the claims adjuster assigned to my aircraft insurance claim, asking me to submit all of the documents concerning the theft. It took me a few days to collect all the documents he asked for, and I sent them via US mail to him.

What I didn't know at the time was that Miller, after our first phone conversation, had immediately called the United States Department of Transportation (DOT) and notified a special investigations agent by the name of Mr. Jesse O'Brien that I had setup the theft of an aircraft I had insured with him, and that I was in the process of making a false insurance claim.

Mr. Miller was pleasant, courteous and professional to me and gave me no indications to suspect that there was a problem with the insurance claim. Per the insurance contract, at ninety days the insurance company paid my claim of 151,500 dollars for the stolen Cessna T210. I remember clearly telling Mr. Miller over the telephone that I knew where the plane was and what had happened and that I had pictures of the stolen airplane camouflaged in different colors, but he acted surprisingly disinterested. This should have raised a red flag, but at the time I thought nothing of it.

At the time of the theft, I had paid aircraft insurance premiums for more than fifteen years without any claims, but through my experience in dealing with the insurance companies I learned that the aviation insurance industry isn't exactly a group of upstanding citizens either. While I was paying my premiums over the years I was a great guy, but the first time I made a claim and needed them to insure my personal property, which was what I had been paying them to do, I suddenly was an airplane thief. Even though they paid my claim, which by law they had to do, they turned around and reported me to the feds as a thief. They hoped that I'd be found guilty of fraud which would enable them recover their money from the claim.

Other than liability coverage, I haven't insured a personal airplane since the Cessna T210 nor will I ever again.

Chapter 9

The weird stuff starts

"Honey, come home quick, there has been a break in at the house and I am afraid to go inside!" That was my wife calling me from our driveway in Scottsdale, Arizona, in February 2006. I hurried home to find the back door to my house kicked in, and I called the police. The house had not been touched except for my home office, which had been trashed. At the time I thought that we had been the victims of a regular burglary, but as I began to hunt around for what was missing I began to wonder. Nothing of value was taken even though there were two new laptop computers in plain sight, but I noticed many of my aircraft files were gone. Later that day when I turned on my laptop I saw a small, strange popup window I hadn't seen before in the lower right hand screen area. It flashed on and off quickly but I thought I read "United States of America" before it disappeared. Now that was odd. Within a few months of the airplane theft and subsequent insurance claim, a lot of weird stuff started happening. Our telephones at home and work were making funny noises, an indication that they were tapped. We started finding exterior doors of our home left ajar. We would be missing mail from our mailbox. Jenny and I both had people following us everywhere. Finally we had my records concerning the burglary of my aircraft stolen.

One day I received a notice from my bank in the mail saying that they were canceling one of my business lines of credit. I immediately made an appointment with my banker at the local branch to investigate the reason. As I sat down, my banker eyed my up and said, "John, I have a report here from a United States federal agency that says you are involved in fraudulent business activities and, as the responsible party on your account, I have cancelled your credit line to protect the bank's interests."

I said, "Look, I have never made a late payment to your bank, or to anyone else's bank, and I can tell you without hesitation that I am not involved in anything illegal. I have done business at this bank for many years and would like to continue our relationship, but I am going to need a better explanation than the nonsense answer you just gave me."

He knew I wasn't kidding. He leaned over his desk and whispered, "DOT," and then said out loud that he was sorry, but he had another appointment and couldn't do anything else for me.

As I discovered later, that is a typical trick of the feds, they smear you to everyone you know and then put pressure on you both financially and personally. Special DOT Agent O'Brien and his crew eventually made it to everyone even remotely connected with me to spread their lies and to pump them for any information they could. Many of my friends called me wondering what was going on. At the time I told them that I wished I knew. The DOT agents even attacked a plane I sold to a guy while he was on an airport ramp in the state of Iowa, jerked the pilots out of the plane, threw them on the ground and searched them saying that it was a drug smuggling plane and that they were confiscating it. After searching the airplane and finding nothing, the feds didn't confiscate the plane and released the pilots. Needless to say, guys that I sold the planes to were not happy with me. Most of them called me on the phone and yelled at me for several minutes at a time telling me their stories about how the feds searched their planes, came to their homes or followed them. I couldn't believe what I was hearing from them, but it was true; they had no reason to lie.

Abuse of Power

Chapter 10

Raid by the feds

October 20, 2006, 0800

"Everybody freeze! If anyone moves, you're dead!" That was a the voice of a man I came to know as US DOT Special Agent Jesse O'Brien. He was shouting orders at five of us as he lead several bullet proof jacketed, armed agents storming the aircraft maintenance facility of Mustang aviation at the Scottsdale Arizona Airport.

Work usually started at the Mustang maintenance hangar in Scottsdale at about 0800. Unlike most mornings, which were relatively uneventful, this day brought unexpected mayhem. I had planned on being in the hangar early to check on a plane that the Mustang crew was working on for me. I had only been there for about fifteen minutes when I saw several unmarked black cars screeching to a halt outside of the main hangar doors blocking us all inside. A team of armed federal agents stormed in with guns drawn and ordered all five of us to the center of the hangar. I counted twenty of them. It reminded me of a scene from a movie, only this was for real. I didn't particularly want to die that morning, so I did what they said. If it wasn't such a serious situation, I would have laughed. The way these agents stormed in, all jacked up on adrenaline, you would have thought we were number one on the Most Wanted List.

Those agents came in armed and ready to fire, and I was familiar with cases where they have accidentally killed more than a few innocent people. Thank goodness we were spared that inconvenience.

The agents separated us into groups, one of us for every three agents. My three agents asked me to sit down and wait, and I obeyed. A man came walking over to me and introduced himself as Special Agent Jesse O'Brien. He was a short, slightly overweight man in his mid-thirties with thinning brown hair. He asked my name, address and phone number. These were things he already knew; as I discovered later, a federal agent will only ask questions he already knows the answers to, or at least thinks he knows the answers to, in order to ascertain if you are going to lie. He explained that he was a special aviation investigator with the DOT. Immediately I had my doubts he had investigated much of anything because if he had, he would have discovered that nobody in the Mustang facility had done anything worse than incuring a few traffic violations. Next he asked if I could tell him about a Cessna T210 I had purchased from the Mustang facility. I said that I of course could.

He responded, "It would be better if we could meet in your office in Scottsdale." I agreed and he said he would call me to arrange the meeting in the near future. He said I was free to go. I left as they began confiscating the aircraft logbooks, records and aircraft that were in the hangar.

After all the agents had left and while I was walking to my car, I received a call from my insurance claims adjuster, Joe Miller. There had not been any communication from him since the insurance claim was paid on the Cessna T210 some time ago and I thought the timing was quite odd. Joe said, "Hello Johnny, how are you this morning?"

I didn't catch his sarcasm at first and answered, "Honestly not so well."

He said, "Yeah I know and now I am going to screw you like you screwed me!" and hung up.

As I was driving home an hour later, I kept thinking how extraordinarily bizarre his comments were, but I didn't have a clue how much worse it was going to get.

Chapter 11

Threats from the DOT

November 20 2006

Special agent O'Brien called me almost a month later on my cell phone and asked to meet me at 1000 hours in my office at the Scottsdale airport. He showed up on time with a big notebook and two DEA agents who identified themselves as Agents Harper and Rowe. Now I wish that I had had an attorney sitting there, but I knew I hadn't done anything wrong and at the time didn't know any better. I didn't know what they were going to ask me, but I wasn't too worried about it either. Agent O'Brien started out by asking if I knew about the Cessna T210 stolen in Mexico.

I replied, "Of course I do. It was my airplane and I was there."

He then came right out and said, "Look, Mr. Mack don't play games with me. I can prove that you did not even own that airplane and that you setup the theft of it and submitted a false insurance claim which is a felony."

Right then I should have shut up and closed the meeting but his statement was so ridiculous it made me angry and I started talking, which is exactly what he wanted.

I said, "Mr. O'Brien you are wrong on both counts, and I don't care for the fact you come in here with these accusations. I understand the fact that getting an airplane stolen in Mexico may look bad to you, but it's no different than getting one stolen in the United States and I had insurance coverage for both countries."

At this point one of the DEA agents spoke up and said, "Mr. Mack we have been watching your aircraft flying across the US-Mexico border for several years now, and I think you should be even more worried about that."

I could see that this was heading downhill for me. I said, "Look, I have nothing to hide. Yes, I fly across that border very frequently, but I cross in full compliance of United States and Mexican law, the laws you guys created. Please show me where I have failed to comply with any Federal Aviation Regulation or United States customs law, and I will discuss it with you. Other than that I don't have much else to say."

Agent O'Brien spoke up again and said, "Mr. Mack, I will be arresting you for felony insurance fraud at some point in the near future. It's going to take me a few months but I am going to get you."

One of the DEA guys stepped in and said, "Look I know you are flying drugs across the border and we are going to get you too."

I told them, "Look, both of you are way off base. Yes, I run legitimate businesses in Mexico, and no, I don't smuggle nor would I for any amount of money."

O'Brien then, finally, told me the real reason he came to see me. He said, "Listen, I know you do business with Mustang and they are in big trouble. I can prove they are repairing aircraft with uncertified parts and I am going to indict them for falsifying documents to the FAA over numerous aircraft including the Cessna T210. I will leave you alone if you can give me information to help prosecute them."

It was true that I had done business with Mustang for almost five years, and I had been around their operation enough to know that they were on the up-and-up. I said, "Hey, I have done business with these guys for quite awhile and if you need someone to help prosecute them then you are talking to the wrong guy. Contrary to your allegations against them, I know how they operate. I put my life in these guys' hands almost every time I fly, and I am sorry but you are wrong about them. What would you like me to do? Make up a story about them?"

Not surprisingly O'Brien responded, "That would be a good start." I had already said too much; I was done talking and they knew it.

The lesson here is to never talk to a federal agent without an attorney present. Pay the attorney and let him deal with them. The feds are great at spinning webs of lies and that's exactly what O'Brien did out of the few things I said. I also realized that O'Brien had already decided who was guilty and really wasn't interested in discovering any true facts about the case, especially if the facts didn't match his story.

The meeting ended and O'Brien and his crew left. I learned later that for the next few days they met with and threatened everybody I knew or had sold aircraft to and told them I was a drug trafficker. The federal agents also left each one of my business contacts with the threat that they better not associate with me again unless they wanted trouble. If they did not cooperate with the federal agents they too would be risking federal prosecution.

When I left my meeting with O'Brien, I walked directly to my car and drove right to my attorney's office. As I relayed the whole story to my attorney that afternoon, he told me to never talk directly to a fed from this point on, to quit using my phone and email accounts and that he was going to refer me to a criminal defense attorney who could handle my case.

The next afternoon I was sitting in the Scottsdale law office of David Meyers, explaining the whole situation. Mr. Meyers listened to the whole story before commenting, "This sounds to me like it's going to become a big problem in your future, but unfortunately we can't do much about it until they arrest, charge or indict you. I simply cannot defend you over threats."

He explained further that when a federal agency gets a warrant to raid a house or a business, they virtually never get arrests or indictments that are related to how they got the warrant for search in the first place. A federal agent can go directly to a federal judge with a complaint he has fabricated even if it's total supposition and get the judge to sign an arrest or search warrant. The agent is betting that once he gets inside the search target he will find something to prosecute on, even if it's completely unrelated to his initial warrant. He also said that the feds have a 98% conviction rate; in other words they always win. Whether through prosecution or plea bargain, they are virtually impossible to beat on their own court. This wasn't sounding too good for me, but Mr. Meyers continued, "This agent is on a fishing expedition right now and he is standing over your pond. There is no telling what he can and will do, but I will warn you now, you better watch your step because these guys will lie, cheat or steal to win their case. I do this for a living and I would put nothing past them."

Abuse of Power

Chapter 12

The Patriot act and you

I include my own brief synopsis of the Patriot Act only to help you understand the constitutional abuses it encompasses. Like many Americans, I did not read the Patriot Act when it was enacted because I assumed it was written to go get the bad guys, the terrorists who committed the atrocities of September 11, 2001. When I saw it being used against me, a United States of America born citizen, I dug it up and read it, and I personally recommend that you read it too. It is an overthrow of the United States Constitution by the United States Government with the ultimate goal of taking away your constitutional rights, not those of terrorists.

The United States of America Patriot Act, commonly known as the Patriot Act, is a statute enacted by the Government of the United States that was then signed into law by President George W. Bush on October 26, 2001. The acronym (US PATRIOT) stands for Uniting and Strengthening America by Providing Appropriate Tools Required to Intercept and Obstruct Terrorism. The Act basically increases the ability of law enforcement agencies to search telephone, email, medical, financial and other records. It also enhances the discretion of law enforcement in detaining and deporting both United States citizens and illegal immigrants suspected of terrorism related acts. The Act also expands the definition of terrorism to include domestic terrorism, thus enlarging the number of activities to which the Patriot Act's expanded law enforcement powers can be applied. Opponents of the law frequently criticize the Act's authorization for indefinite detentions of persons, searches of a home or business without the owner's permission or knowledge and the expanded use of National Security Letters, which allow agencies to search telephone, email and financial records without a court order. There have been a few legal challenges against the act, and federal courts have ruled that a number its provisions are unconstitutional.

I also would like to offer my brief synopsis on Title II of the Patriot Act, which is entitled Enhanced Surveillance Procedures. This title covers all aspects of the surveillance of suspected terrorists or anyone engaged in clandestine activities. It allows government agencies to gather foreign intelligence information from both United States citizens and non-citizens. This title removes the legal wall between criminal investigations and surveillance and also allows surveillance to be carried out on anyone at anytime. Before the Patriot Act, the government would have to prove they had a reason to begin surveillance on an individual before surveillance started. Now they are able to do it to anyone without proving cause. The Title also gives authorities the ability to share information gathered before a federal grand jury with other agencies.

Wiretapping orders are also expanded under Title II. They were expanded to include addressing and routing information to allow surveillance of packet switched networks. The Act allowed any district court judge in the United States to issue such orders and search warrants for terrorism investigations. Search warrants were also expanded to stored voicemail, pen registers and trap and trace devices. The last was installed on my computer during the break in. It also entitles the government, through your cable company, to view your phone calls, session times on your computer, your bank and credit card info and even your cable TV viewing habits if there is supposed danger to life and limb. It also established the government's right to sneak and peak warrants and roving wiretaps and any government agency's right to gain access to documents that reveal the patterns of US citizens.

A sneak and peak is simply an indefinitely delayed notification of search warrant. You get searched by the feds first and then notified about it at a later date.

Correct me if I am wrong but is that not a violation of our Fourth Amendment rights? As a Reminder, the Fourth Amendment to the Constitution is our protection as citizens of the United States from unreasonable search and seizure by our government. Maybe someone should remind our legislators about it.

Roving wiretaps violate the same Fourth Amendment rights and allow agencies to spy on cell phone calls without a warrant. Once a law like this is enacted, these agencies are obligated to test it. They probably do a lot more testing than we think. I do not believe the United States Government has the right to violate the Constitution, but they sure gave themselves the authority to violate it through the Patriot Act.

What next? It also allows the FBI specifically to seize the production of, or remove from any public library, any tangible items such as books, records and documents to protect us against international terrorism as they see fit.

Does this sound like abuse of power?

Chapter 13

Arrested

February 21 2008

I flew back to Arizona from Mexico in the afternoon. I cleared United States customs in Nogales, Arizona, and proceeded on to Glendale, Arizona, airport where I had left a car. As I drove home, I noticed a white economy car seemed to be following me, but it stayed just far enough behind me so that I couldn't see the occupants. I knew that I had been tailed before by the feds, so I didn't think about it too much. The drive to my house in Scottsdale took about forty-five minutes in traffic and, other than being followed, was uneventful. I had just closed the front door to my house and kissed my wife hello when there was a knock at the door. Almost fourteen months had passed since O'Brien's promise to arrest me, and personally I believed that he would do it. I lived with the uncertainty of when and how it was going to happen. I wasn't at all surprised when I answered the front door and Agent O'Brien was standing there with a frightened looking postal inspector. With a big grin on his face, O'Brien asked me to step outside and ordered me to put my hands behind my back so he could handcuff me. I obeyed. He made quite a show of my arrest. He purposefully paraded me around my front yard in view of my neighbors, my wife and my children. He had convinced himself that he had bagged a big trophy and, like a little kid, wanted to brag about it. I finally got into the back seat of the white economy car that had followed me and he literally started calling his friends on his cell phone saying, "Yeah I got him. I told you I would!"

Once we were about ten minutes from my house O'Brien turned to me and said, "Hey look, I don't think you're a bad guy. I think you just are in over your head and scared. Tell me something about Mustang maintenance and I will let you go tonight."

I didn't have much to say to him. I had been arrested without being read my rights and they wouldn't even tell my wife or me where they were taking me.

O'Brien took my cell phone from me during the arrest and gave it to my wife saying to her, "you need to read through his text messages." The government had had my phone tapped for two years as I suspected. What O'Brien knew that my wife didn't was that I had been unfaithful in my marriage, and he knew he could probably get her to testify against me if she was upset and vindictive. My attorney had warned me they would use whatever they could, right or wrong, to get a conviction.

I have long since accepted that my behavior in my marriage was inexcusable. I have repented and overcome it. O'Brien and the postal inspector drove me to the Tempe, Arizona, city jail and threw me in a small cell. O'Brien said that I was a federal detainee, which at the time meant nothing to me. I sat down in a state of confusion and waited.

About an hour later I was taken to an interview room. O'Brien walked in and said, "Look, I know and I can prove that you got paid twice for that Cessna T210 airplane."

I said, "How is that?" He proceeded to pull my bank records out and point to a 197,000-dollar transaction crediting my bank account only a few weeks before the theft of the Cessna T210 and then showed me the deposits from the insurance check that I deposited to the same account months later.

I saw his problem immediately and said, "I hope you didn't build your case on that information, Mr. O'Brien."

I could see that upset him, but he responded, "What do you mean?"

I pointed to the statement and said, " Do you see the escrow account number on that first transaction? It says Mooney N252Y. That is a totally different airplane that I had sold to a buyer from California." It was the Mooney airplane I had sold just before the theft of the Cessna T210.

O'Brien looked somewhat puzzled and said, "Well, I will be checking on that for sure."

I knew at that point I wasn't dealing with the sharpest tool in the shed, but that made him far more dangerous. Before he left the interview room he mentioned he had traveled to Sonora and Sinaloa, Mexico, and had people ready to testify that I was supplying aircraft to the Mexican drug cartels. I knew that he was lying on that point. If an agent like O'Brien showed up in Sinaloa looking for airplanes and drugs and found them, the chance that he would see the light of day again would be remote at best. He would stick out like a mustard seed in a tar pit. The people down there down there aren't real friendly toward USA law enforcement types and more than likely wouldn't think twice before making him disappear.

After the interview I was escorted to a new cell with four detainees in it. I managed to get a little sleep before the federal agents returned for me early the next morning. Since my arrest I had been given no food or water and I wasn't allowed to make a phone call. They drove me to the federal court building in Phoenix in an unmarked car and one of them said to me, "This is your last chance. We've got you cold and your life as you know it is over. Are you going to go down for those guys at Mustang?"

By that time I knew better than to talk to them anyway, and I remained silent. They marched me in front of a federal judge with a group of Mexican illegal aliens. At this point I still didn't even know why I had been arrested.

Inside the courtroom, an assistant district attorney for Arizona stood up and she quickly read O'Brien's paperwork to the judge. The judge then announced just as quickly that, "based on the statement from Agent O'Brien, I deem you to be an extreme flight risk and a threat to United States National Security and recommend you be incarcerated in the federal facility at Florence until we can reconvene at a later date."

I had never been arrested before and was shocked that I was not being released on my own recognizance as my court appointed attorney had expected. My court appointed attorney Alex, who spent all of one minute with me before the hearing had said, "You have never even been arrested before, and you are going home today." Boy was he ever wrong! My attorney was as surprised as I was and responded to the judge by simply asking, "Are you kidding?"

It was obvious to me that this was a theatrical act, not a court of law in the United States of America and that all of this had been planned by the feds. I also understood the reason why they arrested me on a Thursday. As they knew, it meant that the next hearing would be postponed until the next week and hopefully much longer, giving them more time to break me.

Next I was escorted, along with thirty Mexican

illegal aliens, out of the courtroom and put in a cell for a strip search. We were given federal prisoner uniforms, and then the guards cuffed our hands and shackled our feet. We shuffled down some narrow hallways to an underground, secure bus loading area. The ride from Phoenix to Florence is about an hour and a half, but it seemed like three days while we looked out the windows of the bus watching everyone going out for their Friday night activities while we went to prison. It seemed surreal and ugly.

We arrived at the federal facility in Florence, Arizona, unloaded from the bus and herded into another large room. Initially it seemed large, but it became so crammed with inmates, arriving from all over the place, that it was standing room only. This room was filthy and full of all sorts of people. There were junkies throwing up all over the place from drug detoxification sickness. There were fights breaking out. It was just hell in general. I met a few illegal Mexicans standing near me and found out that they were from Sonora. I knew some people from their families, and we began talking. It helped pass the time. The guards finally sorted us out, gave us numbers and marched us through group showers. We were each assigned a bag with some clothes and a shower kit, then they herded us through a medical exam and shot us up with who knows what. This took almost seven hours. We finally got to our cells about 0300 and went to sleep.

Breakfast call is at 0600, and that is when your cell door is unlocked. After breakfast we were free to roam around in a large room, but at night were locked in our cells with our cellmates. I don't need to tell you that prison food isn't great, but you couldn't tell from the way some of the guys ate. In prison you always eat meals with your race, so I sat with the white guys in my cellblock. They were all in for federal drug charges and they wanted to know what I was doing there. I told them my story and they thought I was making it up, but it was the truth and I wasn't going to make up stories for them. Many of the Mexicans in our cellblock found out I spoke Spanish and some of them came over and asked me to translate their paperwork. The funny thing was, I had no paperwork. I still had not been presented with paperwork from my own case, and I wondered what was going on. Jenny finally got copies of the paperwork a few days later, and it included a federal complaint that O'Brien made against me. I was finally able to talk with her over the phone to tell her that I was fine. She knew they had taken me to Florence, but that was about it.

I was able to keep fairly busy translating paperwork for the Mexicans. I remember shortly after I was transferred to Florence, a Mexican prisoner that I hadn't met before walked over and tried to befriend me with small talk. "Oye guero," he said, which means hey white boy, "I have some airplanes in Mexico that have been crashed or confiscated by the Mexican federalies, but I can make arrangements to get them to you very cheap." I looked at him and smiled. He continued, "What do you say? I have all the connections down there."

I turned around and walked away. Even I was surprised the feds were this stupid. Are you kidding? Yeah, I am going to make a deal to buy airplane parts while I am sitting here in federal prison accused of drug trafficking and fraud and who knows what else.

He approached me again later with the same story, but I told him that I wasn't interested in airplanes but wanted to import furniture from Guadalajara. He looked at me sort of funny then smiled and said, "OK my friend, we will talk later." He finally left me alone.

I spent the next few days talking with my cellmates, learning about them. One was a fifty-year-old Mexican national from Oaxaca, named Jorge who had been through this process before. He taught me how the immigration system worked. He would come across the United States border, work awhile, get picked up and do a month in the federal prison – where you are fed and taken care of medically – then get deported and start the whole process over again. He was a decent guy with a boxing background and he taught my other cellmate and I exercises we could do in the cell to keep us fit. Julio was my other cellmate, and his story was a little different. One of his vehicles had been caught with two tons of cocaine in it, and he was facing some hard time. He must have been a fairly large-scale trafficker, because he had been in the process of facial reconstruction when they picked him up so he could change his identity. He was still recovering from his last surgery when he arrived in the Federal prison. He had been born in the United States but spoke Spanish very well. We mostly communicated in Spanish in the cell because the older guy with us didn't speak English, and we didn't want to be rude. We passed the time playing cards and talking, and it amazed me how much you can learn about someone in such a short time when that's all there is to do.

Chapter 14

Club fed release

February 26 2008.

The guards buzzed me out of my cell at 0300 the next morning. My two cellmates said buena suerte, which means good luck, and I was taken to a holding area with other prisoners to wait for the bus. We were driven back the same way we had come to the federal court building in Phoenix, and when we arrived there we were subjected to another strip search. My court appointed attorney had phoned my wife to bring clothes in case they released me this time and to my surprise they did. My father had shown up at the court building and almost blew his lid when he met Agent O'Brien face to face in the hallway. Thank goodness Dad ended up being satisfied with giving O'Brien the stare down! In fact, my whole family as well as Jenny's had shown up in my support. They pretty much filled the courtroom, which seemed to annoy O'Brien. After some last minute antics by O'Brien and the prosecution in the attempt to keep me locked up until another hearing could be convened, the judge released me on the conditions of surrendering my United States passport

and signing a bond for 25,000 dollars to guarantee
I would appear in federal court in San Francisco,
California, on a future date. I didn't run before and
certainly wasn't going to run now. The court also put
me under surveillance, which means I had to notify an
appointed officer every time I was going somewhere
away from my house. It was an inconvenience, but it
was better than being locked up. As I was escorted out
of the courtroom, I happened to see the District judge
in a heated argument with agent O'Brien. I don't know
what was said, but O'Brien was getting reprimanded,
surely about my case. That gave me a lot of hope for
my upcoming trial. I was escorted to a changing room
where they removed my handcuffs and leg irons. I
changed into my street clothes and found my way out of
the courthouse.

There were plenty of tears as we were all reunited
outside of the federal court building where my family
had been waiting for me. It had only been a week since
my arrest, but it had certainly felt like much longer. We
went to lunch where we talked about my adventure, and
then we headed for home to prepare the real work of
winning my freedom.

Chapter 15

Hired Gun

As soon as Jenny and I arrived home that day, I wanted to see the paperwork O'Brien had generated about me. We sat down at the kitchen table and started going over it. It is a sobering feeling when you are staring at official paperwork from the United States of America saying you are involved in terrorist activities, a threat to United States National Security and just an all around bad guy. At first I didn't fully understand how any of this was even possible or constitutional, as I was sure my rights had been violated on several counts. I finally came upon the phrase "under the Patriot Act" in my paperwork, and that got my attention.

In his ultimate wisdom, and in his rush to prosecute because the statute of limitations was running out on my case, O'Brien had classified my business activities as "terrorist in nature" and was able to apply all the abuses of the Patriot Act to my civil rights. In short, he never needed search warrants to break into my office, tap my phones, take my bank records or install software on my computer, so he could spy on me as well as read my email. O'Brien wrote up a formal complaint against me concerning his theory that I had set up the theft of my Cessna T210. While reading the complaint I came across the statement, "Mr. Mack even admitted that his future didn't look good." which was of course something he twisted from what I had said during our meeting and turned into something that simply was not the truth. From his complaint of sheer supposition as well as out and out lies, Agent O'Brien was able to get a federal judge to sign an arrest warrant against me, a document I was just seeing for the first time. The simple fact that an agent can get an arrest warrant so easily is just plain wrong, especially because if the agent is incorrect with his accusation the damage has been done and the agent has no accountability for his eagerness to prosecute someone, innocent or guilty. They have the attitude, "Oh, sorry, too bad I destroyed your reputation, see you later."

If that isn't bad enough, what about never being read my rights?

What about illegal search and seizure?

What about being innocent until proven guilty?

I had no experience with the legal system up to this point in my life but this certainly was not what I had expected. It was an awaking and alarming experience. One of the first things I needed was a good criminal defense attorney in the San Francisco area where I was to be appearing in court. I had a recommendation from my attorney, a criminal defense lawyer named Gary Goldstein, in the Bay area. I relayed my story to him and after I was finished he said that he had never heard a story like mine, but he agreed to take me on as a client.

My wife and I flew up to San Francisco on March 30, 2008, and met with Gary Goldstein in his law office. I liked Gary immediately. He was a sixty-year-old tall, thin Jewish man that had been around the legal scene in the Bay area for most of his life and had defended many big cases in his career. I re-told Gary the whole story, this time in more detail, and he said, "I like your case but I am going to warn you that this isn't going to be a quick process or a cheap one. These guys think they have you on something or it wouldn't have gotten this far. I have set up an appointment in one hour to meet the prosecuting attorney of your case, so let's go see what he wants from you."

Gary's office was located only a block from the federal building, so Gary, Jenny and I decided to walk over there. As we were walking, Gary began to explain how a federal case works. He said his biggest worry was that once an investigation like this starts, somebody's head has to roll whether the government is right or not, and one way or the other the government virtually always gets their way. They have unlimited financial resources, man power and whatever else they need to drag you into bankruptcy, even if they know they are wrong. Our challenge was to stop them in their tracks before this mess got any bigger. Suddenly we were standing on the steps of the federal building, and it was time to go in. We went through security and took an elevator to one of the upper floors where we met a security guard who escorted us to the prosecutor's office. The door was opened, and we walked in. Gary introduced us to the prosecutor. He was a small, thin older man who hesitantly shook my hand. His name was James Stuckey, and he had been a prosecuting attorney for the government for thirty years.

We all sat down and Mr. Stuckey began. "Mr. Goldstein, your client is a dangerous criminal, and I intend to indict him this week on charges ranging from insurance fraud to drug trafficking. I intend to come at Mr. Mack with every weapon the government possesses including the IRS, and I will have an indictment by the end of the week and a conviction by the end of the year."

Gary spoke up and said, "What percentage would you put on your case against Mr. Mack that you will convict him in front of a jury?"

Mr. Stuckey replied, "Ninety-five percent."

Gary replied, "Well it looks like I have some work to do, and I would like you to grant me two weeks to explain Mr. Mack's side of the story before you move to an indictment.

Mr. Stuckey agreed and added, "I will drop my case today against Mr. Mack if he agrees to testify against the owners of Mustang Maintenance."

Gary nodded his head, smiled politely and suddenly the meeting was over.

As we were walking back to his office, Gary asked what I thought about the threats by Stuckey. I told him I wasn't even sure what evidence Stuckey could possibly have against me to indict me on any charges, let alone convict me. Gary said, "Well, they don't really need any evidence to get an indictment from a grand jury because the grand jury only hears the government's side of the story whether it's right or wrong. If they indict you, I will have to change my defense strategy for you, and an indictment in itself is pretty meaningless. I am going to try to stop them before they move to indictment, but I make no guarantees. I have gone up against Stuckey many times in court and have never lost a case to him, but I haven't seen him this aggressive before. I am going to need a retainer of 40,000 dollars, and that is just to cover you up to a trial if it goes that far."

I wrote Gary a check for that amount and Jenny and I flew back to Phoenix.

One of the first things I had Gary work on was recovering my United States Passport, which I had surrendered to the court. I couldn't work without it, and Gary was able to get it back for me within a few weeks. I traveled back and forth to San Francisco a few times to make preliminary court appearances, but those hearings were just formalities and nothing much happened. I did learn that in general terms, attorneys all sit down together and decide how court proceedings are going to go so there are no real surprises during a hearing.

Federal court is no joke and, I don't have to tell you, I didn't like being there. The stress of it all was starting to take a toll on me, and I constantly had to beat down thoughts of suicide so my family and I wouldn't be dragged through that mess. I actually sat down one evening and wrote up my last will and testament. I became so depressed over everything that I got up early the next morning with a plan to end it all. I had decided to go for a hike through the mountains near my house, climb the highest cliff and jump into oblivion. It was a beautiful spring day and I enjoyed every meter of my hike into the mountains, taking extra time to notice the beauty around me because I knew I wasn't going to see it again. As I reached the mountain summit, I felt better than I had in months. I took a long look at the Valley of the Sun and stepped toward the edge of the cliff. There were plenty of loose rocks and this would probably even look like an accident. I saw the first part of the mountain my body would hit and figured it was more than five hundred feet below me.

I started to lean forward and heard a small voice that seemed to come from behind me saying, "What are you doing?" Surprised, I turned around expecting to see someone there, but I saw no one. The voice continued and it was then I realized it was coming from inside my head. It said in soft but steady words, "Why would you quit now? You have come this far and you are going to throw it all away? What about your wife? What about your kids and your family? They are here supporting you to the very end, and you want to betray them like this? It's your choice, but suicide is a coward's choice, and you are not a coward. Don't worry about the idiots from the government. They know they are wrong and so do you." I suddenly recognized the voice; it was that of my grandfather who died several years earlier. I knew he was right, and I turned away from the cliff and started walking back down the mountain.

For the next few weeks, Gary went back and forth with Stuckey and O'Brien. He had finally beat O'Brien's complaint down so badly to Stuckey that Stuckey stated to Gary, "The government's case lacks any real evidence. I have no confidence in O'Brien's investigative work, and he also appears to have no clue what he is doing."

This was good news for us, but as Gary explained to me a government's case unfortunately couldn't end just because they figured out that they were wrong. The government had tied up nearly five years and millions of dollars in this investigation, and they are going to want something more.

All along, O'Brien had wanted me to submit to a polygraph test that he would administrate, even though polygraphs are not admissible in court. That was not going to happen, but it gave Gary an idea. Gary proposed to Stuckey that if I submitted to a government administered polygraph test and passed it, the government would drop the investigation against me as well as any further legal action. O'Brien was all for it because he was sure I was lying and was under the impression that he would be involved in the polygraph test. Stuckey just wanted to save face at this point and agreed to the deal. Gary called me and relayed what he had arranged, and I was happy to take the test. I had never taken a polygraph test before, but I really had nothing to hide so I was eager to take it.

Gary told Stuckey that he wanted the questions in writing that would be asked before the test so he could review them and their legality as they pertained to the case and his client. This was not going to be an O'Brien fishing inquest, and Gary would make sure of it. What Gary didn't tell them was that he had hired a different government agency to administer the test.

After receiving the questions in writing, Gary flew down to Phoenix and we drove together to the DEA's polygraphist office on May 10, 2008. The person administering the test was a twenty-seven year veteran of the DEA with twenty-five years experience administering the tests. The questions were fairly simple. Of course they start with baseline questions like, "What is your name?" and "Did you travel here by car?" to see what your normal reaction is. The questions the government came up with were:

1. Did you purchase a Cessna T210 from Mustang maintenance?

2. Did you make a fraudulent insurance claim for the Cessna T210?

3. Did you setup the theft of the Cessna T210?

4. Did you legally purchase the Cessna T210?

5. Have you ever smuggled narcotics to the United States?

That was it. The polygraphist repeated the series of questions several times, and when the test was over I returned to the front office to wait for Gary.

After a private interview between Gary and the polygraphist, we left the testing office and I drove Gary back to the airport to catch his flight. As we were driving, Gary turned to me and said, "The test went great. We have got them now." Gary's' plan had worked. We had used a DEA polygraphist unfamiliar with my case or me, we paid for it ourselves and only Gary and I knew about it. Had the test gone poorly, Gary would have told the feds to rephrase the questions or tried to force them into an indictment, which Stuckey wasn't too keen on doing anyway. However the test went well, and it suddenly felt as if a huge weight was lifting from my shoulders. Gary received the official test results a week later and immediately went over to Stuckey's office to present them to Stuckey and O'Brien. The Polygraphist test results were undeniable, and the Polygraphists reputation and credentials were indisputable. Gary later told me that Stuckey and O'Brien sat in their chairs absolutely dumbfounded when they realized what he had done, and I am sure they sat there for awhile after he left and tried to figure out how they had gotten so badly bamboozled by Gary.

That was the last straw for Stuckey, and he wanted no more of this mess. He finally gave in and officially closed the investigation with prejudice on June 16, 2008, and included a statement that the government would be continuing to watch Mr. Mack's "illegal activities."

Whatever!

Chapter 16

The feds get raided

Apparently Stuckey wasn't the only one fed up with O'Brien and his crew. Not long after my case closed, the FBI raided the Dallas–Ft. Worth Federal Aviation Administration of the Flight Standards District Office (FSDO), which also happened to be O'Brien's headquarters. It was run by his boss, a man by the name of Fred Adams. O'Brien's team was becoming more and more bold until a Congresswoman from Atlanta, Georgia, finally went to Washington, DC to ask for an investigation because one of her more wealthy constituents had been forced into bankruptcy by O'Brien's team. O'Brien had the man's business line of credit cancelled, just like he did in my case, and caused the failure of a development company in the Atlanta area. The Congresswoman raised enough questions about the federal agents and their ethics to start a congressional investigation and ultimately succeeded in cutting the funding of O'Brien's group.

The FBI's raid of the Dallas-Ft, Worth FSDO was big news, and they ultimately arrested and prosecuted O'Brien's boss for destroying case evidence. With his world crumbling, O'Brien ducked for cover. Seeing his boss arrested must have been a wake up call because he went into a full retreat when he realized what was happening, but this was far from over.

Chapter 17

Bruce Kelly

I met Bruce Kelly after my federal court case was over when he responded to an aircraft for sale ad I placed for a Cessna 182. Bruce and I agreed to meet at the Chandler, Arizona, airport where I was keeping the airplane. Bruce showed up with his two children and looked over the airplane. He seemed like a nice guy and was very excited about getting his pilot's license and buying his own airplane. Bruce said he worked for the State of Arizona, which didn't seem right to me but I took him at his word. I thought he looked like a federal agent and so did Jenny who was with me that day. You have to remember that at this time my case had been dropped but the Mustang Maintenance trial was still pending, and I was very aware of the fact that Agent O'Brien could still be trying to make his case against me. It was also possible that I was skeptical of people because of my experience. In any case I trusted Bruce. I showed him the report of the annual inspection of the Cessna 182 that Mustang had signed off on, and after I took Bruce on a test flight, he bought the airplane.

Over the next few months I flew with Bruce a few times in between his flight lessons and got to know him a lot better. He finally did admit that he had connections with federal agencies. He said that he had not mentioned it before because he thought it made people nervous, and I couldn't really blame him for that after what I had gone through. Bruce never mentioned much more about his job, and I didn't ask. I liked Bruce, but deep inside I had a feeling he was some sort of setup guy for O'Brien. I wasn't worried because I wasn't doing anything wrong. Bruce promised me that he was on the level and that he only was there because he had big dreams of flying his wife and kids to different places, especially in Mexico, and asked if I would go with them on their first trip down to Mexico, which I gladly agreed to do.

Spending time with Bruce helped me understand that he was a good family man, and I realized that not all government employees are necessarily bad people. A month before the Mustang trial I got a call from a friend saying that Bruce had been suddenly killed on the job in a helicopter accident. The news completely shocked me. I attended Bruce's funeral services where Arizona Governor Janet Napolitano delivered the eulogy. I had felt all along that the feds were going to somehow try to use Bruce to testify against Mustang or even me. I believe that Bruce refused to testify, and the feds thought it was better that he simply disappeared.

The timing of everything related to Bruce was just too coincidental for me to ignore.

A year later, Bruce's widow sold the Cessna 182 to a man from Mesa, Arizona. The man told me later that when they went to the bank to complete the deal, she completely fell apart. Bruce is survived by his wife and two young children.

Chapter 18

life goes on

If I thought going up against the government was difficult, I had a lot of repair work to do at home that would make my legal problems seem insignificant. After the stress of the United State's case against me had subsided I had to go back to work. With the absoluteness and seriousness of the case, I had spent a lot of money and time defending myself and hadn't been taking care of things on the home front, both business and personal, and they were in trouble.

Because of the destruction of my reputation, my aircraft business was worthless. I went back to contract flying private jets to survive economically. As the economy sank and the immediate future seemed bleak, I decided to take a job that had been offered to me as a chief pilot for a small Chicago based charter jet operator. It was the first time I had worked for a company that I did not own in my entire life, but I did not mind. I felt blessed to have my freedom and my family after all I went through.

Jenny went through hell, more than I did I believe. During these last years, through my legal problems as well as my unfaithfulness which were both very tough on her, she stood by me. Now we are rebuilding our lives in Chicago. I cannot explain why she decided to stick with me after all I put her through, but I am eternally grateful to her for her patience and long suffering. One thing is for sure, and it is that I will always love her. She has taught me the meaning of unconditional love.

Chapter 19

Mustang wins

February 21, 2009

After one and a half weeks of a federal trial in Oklahoma City, Oklahoma, a year to the day after I was falsely arrested, a federal jury acquitted Mustang on all counts. The prosecutor was the same district attorney that had prosecuted Timothy McVeigh. Just to put that into perspective, the federal government almost never gets beat in its own court. The district attorney that tried the case even has a street named after him near the federal building in Oklahoma City! If there ever were a kangaroo court, this would have been it. The feds knew they had to stack the deck because they flat out had no case. The problem is that most people will not fight the federal government. Mustang, believing in their innocence, had the will to go through with the trial, which in itself is a frightening proposition. The officers of the company risked imprisonment for up to twenty-five years. Taking into account that these individuals were at an advanced age, that sentence might as well have been a death sentence. Even though the federal prosecutor tried to make a plea bargain with

Mustang, the representatives of the company made it clear that there would be no bargaining. They knew the government had no case and were willing to endure the government's harassment for almost five years to ensure that they had their day in court.

During the course of the trial, the government failed to produce facts and witnesses. Mustang's attorneys successfully rebuffed all of the government's moves.

The simple fact is that Mustang had been in the airplane business for over fifty years and followed the rules. The government hung its case on the hope that Mustang would plead out. In the end the jury saw through all the lies in the government's case and acquitted Mustang on all counts. The judge who tried the case even scolded the prosecution afterwards saying they didn't even try the case under the correct United States Code for the charges they were trying to prosecute.

Chapter 20

Notes from the case

The day I was arrested at my house our mail lady came to the front door and asked my wife if I was there so I could sign for a certified letter from the federal government. This should have tipped us off that there was something wrong but it didn't, and I only found out later that there was no letter.

It's wrong that the average person automatically believes anything that the federal government says. They are not experts on the law. They could have been hired just a few months ago, attended some training, and placed into a job that is way over their heads. Unlike a professional in the private sector they carry no responsibility for their mistakes, which in my case were extremely damaging. Many people have asked me if it is possible to sue for damages. The answer is no. Can you imagine being able to act with no fear of losing your job over incompetence, slander or lawsuits?

I can tell you that that kind of a job does not exist in the private sector. It's a lot like the United States Tax Code. You as an individual are held to a pretty high standard while the government is free to do whatever it wants. They ultimately only answer to themselves, and that is where the system is failing. The double standard is sickening. In my case where the agents were so sure I was doing something wrong but lacked real facts, they caused great damage to me and to my business; they ought to be held liable. I can virtually guarantee situations like mine would never happen if there were some liability on the government's side. There should be some consequences for their actions.

Who is the real enemy?

The real enemy is too much government with too much power. What happened to me is a direct result of under qualified employees of the United States government, people with too much authority, with an austere attitude. It seems that every day we are willfully turning more and more control over to our government. The United States Government is becoming a conglomeration of criminals, and it seems that all they do in Washington, DC is come up with new ways to bilk their citizens out of more money and take away their principle freedoms. Do you not remember that our forefathers revolted and started a war over a tea tax?

The United States of America, the greatest democracy in the history of the world, is being taken over by power mongers and special interests groups. As a proud American citizen, I say it is time for action for we, the people of this country, can change things. We can vote out the elected officials in Washington, DC as well as the local politicians. Most all government officials will overstep their bounds if the people don't hold them accountable. We are in the middle of a great financial crisis and expensive bailout program; we must see to it that our children and grandchildren do not witness such situations in the future.

Our voices and our votes are the only means to end political corruption, and our voices count more than you can even imagine. Apathy is also one of our biggest enemies. Our ancestors built the United States of America with determination and tireless work. The human race has always found a way to survive against difficult odds. The answers to each difficulty are not always simple, yet we must start with the simplest of things, the things we have the power to accomplish, like vote out the politicians who do not reflect our standards and morals and not be blinded by a certain political party.

To avoid disastrous financial situations, we must also live within our means. We must learn to live without things that we cannot afford and so must our government. We must also work to repeal legislation, not create more of it. More legislation begets corruption and chaos. Our elected officials need to understand that we do care and we elect them to support our interests both locally and nationally. They are not elected by us to support special interests and lobbyists. When they realize their tenures will be short lived if they don't represent their constituents, they will shape up or ship out.

I am here to tell you that because of my experiences, I have rededicated myself to being a person of action instead of a person of apathy. I encourage all of you to become involved in your communities and your local government and to vote down any legislation, state or federal, that does not make our respective governments retreat a few steps back towards where they resided a half century ago. We can and must succeed.

The End